STANDARD
OF LIVING

Andrew J. Milson, Ph.D.
Content Consultant
University of Texas at Arlington

Acknowledgments

Grateful acknowledgment is given to the authors, artists, photographers, museums, publishers, and agents for permission to reprint copyrighted material. Every effort has been made to secure the appropriate permission. If any omissions have been made or if corrections are required, please contact the Publisher.

Instructional Consultant: Christopher Johnson, Evanston, Illinois

Teacher Reviewer: Patricia Lewis, Humble Middle School, Humble, Texas

Photographic Credits

Cover, Inside Front Cover, Title Page ©Yu Chu Di/ Redlink/Redlink/Corbis. **3** (bg) ©Stockbyte/Getty Images. **4** (bg) ©Paul Hardy/Corbis. **6** (bg) ©Ludovic Maisant/Hemis/Corbis. **8** (bg) Mapping Specialists. **10** (bg) ©Orlando Barria/epa/Corbis. **11** (tl) Mapping Specialists. **13** (bg) ©Owen Franken/Corbis. **15** (bg) ©Walter Bibikow/JAI/Corbis. **16** (t) ©ADEK BERRY/AFP/Getty Images. **18** (bg) ©Gavin Hellier/ Robert Harding Picture Library Ltd/Alamy. **19** (bl) ©CAREN FIROUZ/Reuters/Corbis. **21** (bg) ©Carlos Cazalis/Corbis. **22** (bg) ©Aaron Kisner courtesy of Vital Voices Global Partnership/ PR NEWSWIRE/Newscom. **22** (cl) ©Philip Andrews/ National Geographic Society. **25** (bg) ©Philip Andrews/National Geographic Society. **27** (t) ©Jim West/Alamy. **28** (tr) ©Photos and Co/Lifesize/Getty Images. **30** (br) ©Walter Bibikow/JAI/Corbis. (tr) ©Roger Eritja/Alamy. **31** (bg) ©Stockbyte/Getty Images. (tr) ©Ludovic Maisant/Hemis/Corbis. (br) ©Paul Hardy/Corbis. (bl) ©ADEK BERRY/AFP/ Getty Images.

MetaMetrics® and the MetaMetrics logo and tagline are trademarks of MetaMetrics, Inc., and are registered in the United States and abroad. The trademarks and names of other companies and products mentioned herein are the property of their respective owners. Copyright © 2010 MetaMetrics, Inc. All rights reserved.

For permission to use material from this text or product, submit all requests online at www.cengage.com/permissions

Further permissions questions can be emailed to permissionrequest@cengage.com

Visit National Geographic Learning online at www.NGSP.com.

Visit our corporate website at www.cengage.com.

Printed in the USA.

RR Donnelley, Menasha, WI

ISBN: 978-07362-97653

15 16 17 18 19 20 21 22

10 9 8 7 6 5 4 3

HOW WE LIV

People who live in the world's most populated areas, such as New York City, New York, in the United States, have access to a vast, complex network of goods and services, but only if they can afford them.

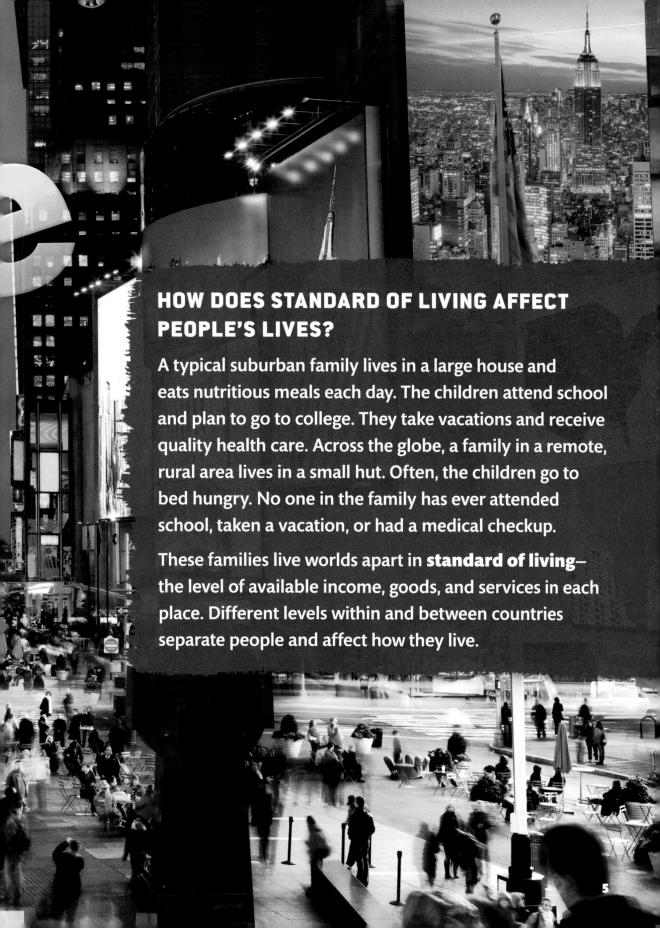

HOW DOES STANDARD OF LIVING AFFECT PEOPLE'S LIVES?

A typical suburban family lives in a large house and eats nutritious meals each day. The children attend school and plan to go to college. They take vacations and receive quality health care. Across the globe, a family in a remote, rural area lives in a small hut. Often, the children go to bed hungry. No one in the family has ever attended school, taken a vacation, or had a medical checkup.

These families live worlds apart in **standard of living**—the level of available income, goods, and services in each place. Different levels within and between countries separate people and affect how they live.

People living below the poverty line would not be able to afford even simple luxuries, such as buying flowers at a popular London street market.

WHAT IS STANDARD OF LIVING?

To measure standard of living, economists look at whether people can afford the basics: clean water, food, shelter, and clothing. Depending on where they live, some people can barely meet their needs while others enjoy luxuries.

Affording the basics depends largely on income, the amount of money a person makes in a certain period of time. A low-wage earner in one country might be a high-wage earner in another because **cost of living** varies from place to place. Cost of living is the amount of money required to maintain a certain standard of living.

Other determining factors include access to education and health care. Level of education influences a person's income. Access to health care affects **life expectancy**, which is the number of years that a person in a particular group or place can expect to live. People with higher standards of living generally live longer lives.

COMPARING STANDARDS OF LIVING

One way to compare standards of living among countries is to look at the number of people living below the poverty line. The **poverty line** is the minimum income required to meet basic needs. The poverty line for a family of four in the United States in 2010 was $22,314. About 15 percent of Americans lived below the poverty line in 2010, compared to 65 percent in Honduras and less than 2 percent in Taiwan.

What do these kinds of statistics say about people's lives? The simplest answer is that the majority of people can meet their basic needs in wealthier countries but not in poorer countries. Next, you'll read about two countries—the Dominican Republic and the United Arab Emirates—with different standards of living and learn how the differences affect people's lives.

Explore the Issue

1. **Summarize** How is standard of living measured?

2. **Analyze Effects** How does standard of living affect people's lives?

COUNTRIES WITH THE HIGHEST STANDARD OF LIVING

1 NORWAY
2 AUSTRALIA
3 NETHERLANDS
4 UNITED STATES
5 NEW ZEALAND
6 CANADA
7 IRELAND
8 LIECHTENSTEIN
9 GERMANY
10 SWEDEN

Source: United Nations HDI 2011 Rankings

Value of all goods produced in a year, divided by a country's population (U.S. Dollars, 2010)

- more than 40,000
- 20,000–39,999
- 10,000–19,999
- 5,000–9,999
- less than 5,000
- no data

NORTH PACIFIC OCEAN

NORTH AMERICA

ALBANIA Many people live in rural poverty, making Albania one of Europe's poorest countries.

NORTH ATLANTIC OCEAN

UNITED STATES Natural resources, a stable political system, and an educated workforce have helped most U.S. citizens to achieve a high standard of living.

CASE STUDY 1

DOMINICAN REPUBLIC The Dominican Republic has been expanding its economy to promote growth in more sectors.

SOUTH AMERICA

SOUTH PACIFIC OCEAN

SOUTH ATLANTIC OCEAN

Explore the Issue

1. **Interpret Maps** What are two continents with countries that produce less than $5,000 per year per person?

2. **Analyze Causes** In countries with higher standards of living, which factors play a role?

und the World

Study the map below to learn about the standard of living in countries around the world.

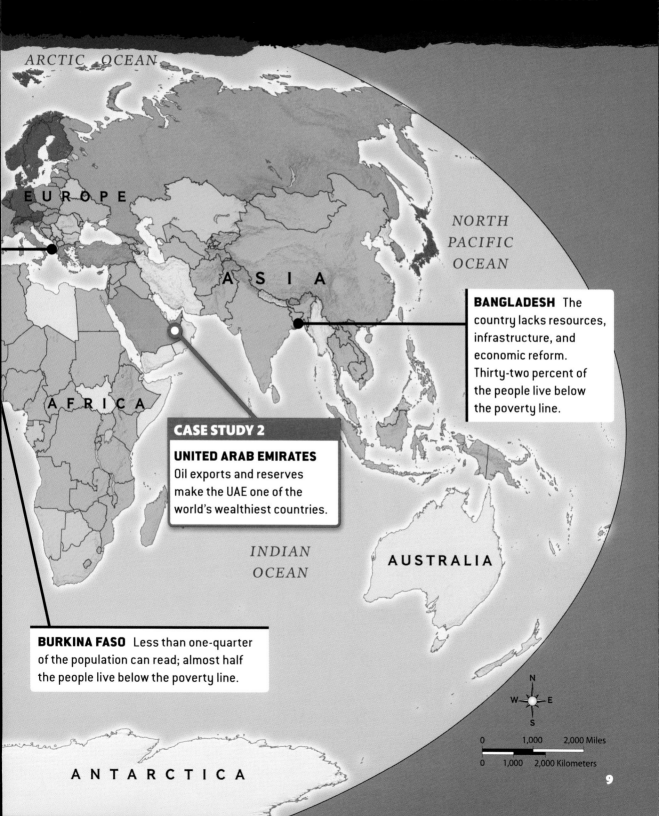

ARCTIC OCEAN

EUROPE

ASIA

AFRICA

NORTH PACIFIC OCEAN

BANGLADESH The country lacks resources, infrastructure, and economic reform. Thirty-two percent of the people live below the poverty line.

CASE STUDY 2

UNITED ARAB EMIRATES
Oil exports and reserves make the UAE one of the world's wealthiest countries.

INDIAN OCEAN

AUSTRALIA

BURKINA FASO Less than one-quarter of the population can read; almost half the people live below the poverty line.

ANTARCTICA

N
W ● E
S

| 0 | 1,000 | 2,000 Miles |
| 0 | 1,000 | 2,000 Kilometers |

Slow Progress in the Dominican Republic

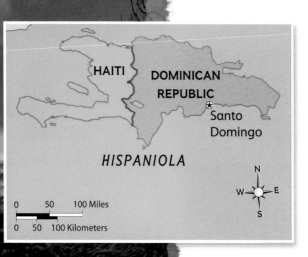

LIGHTS OUT IN SANTO DOMINGO

On February 16, 2010, as people waited to meet the president of the Dominican Republic, the electrical power suddenly failed. For half an hour, the guests stood around in the dark.

The incident illustrates an ongoing challenge for the Dominican Republic, which is on the island of Hispaniola in the Caribbean Sea. The leaders of this developing country want to improve its standard of living. However, persistent power problems slow this progress to a crawl.

As the power outage at the president's palace revealed, the Dominican Republic still needs to develop its **infrastructure**, the system of utilities, roads, and structures that support modern life. In developed countries, having a dependable power grid means industries can develop, produce, and ship products to customers. Residents can power their lights, appliances, and electronics. Power is absolutely essential to boosting a country's standard of living.

FROM DICTATORSHIP TO DEMOCRACY

The Dominican Republic has made some good progress toward improving its standard of living in recent decades. For one thing, it has become a democracy. In the 1800s, it was controlled by Haiti, the country with which it shares Hispaniola. In 1844, after a series of rebellions, the Dominican Republic declared independence.

Dominicans rally at the Ministry of Education Building in Santo Domingo. Protests such as these demonstrate democracy in action.

From 1930 to 1962, the Dominican Republic was ruled by a harsh dictator, Rafael Trujillo (ra-fee-EL troo-HEE-yoh). Following his overthrow, several presidents were elected by the people. Joaquin Balaguer (wah-KEEN bahl-ah-GUR) was elected in 1966 and served multiple terms in office. Under Balaguer, the country made some economic progress. During his third term (1986–1996), he tried to improve infrastructure by building roads, bridges, hydroelectric dams, and other **public works**—government constructed projects for public use. However, these projects plunged the country deeply into debt. In 1996, Dominicans forced Balaguer to step down.

MIXING THINGS UP

However, creating democracy was only one factor on the road to economic development. The Dominican Republic depended too much on agriculture. Sugarcane was its primary crop, with smaller exports of coffee, cacao, and mangos. Depending on only one economic **sector**, or segment of an economy, proved disastrous. If world prices or demand for sugar dropped, for example, the country's economy suffered.

Starting in the late 1990s, the Dominican Republic started to **diversify**, or to develop more economic sectors. For example, the country started to manufacture textiles, clothing, furniture, and consumer goods for export. Exporting products helped the economy because companies hired workers to produce and market products globally.

BOOSTING THE STANDARD OF LIVING

At the same time, the service sector started to take off. Companies that export and import products prospered. Tourism was a bright light, as the country's mild climate, beautiful beaches, and reasonable costs drew thousands of tourists. In addition, the government restored many of the magnificent buildings from the Spanish colonial period.

As the economy developed a broader base, GDP per capita slowly increased. **GDP per capita** is the total value of all goods and services produced in a country in a year, divided by population. As the chart on this page shows, GDP per capita is about 7 times higher than it is in neighboring Haiti, the poorest country in the Western Hemisphere. The Dominican middle class has grown, and the literacy rate has increased to 87 percent. These improvements have helped to reduce some of the **income gap**, or the difference in average wages between rich and poor. As a result, these improvements have helped to raise Dominicans' standard of living.

GDP PER CAPITA FOR SELECTED COUNTRIES IN THE AMERICAS (U.S. DOLLARS, 2011)

COUNTRY	GDP PER CAPITA
United States	48,100
Canada	40,300
Chile	16,100
Mexico	15,100
Brazil	11,600
Dominican Republic	9,300
Paraguay	5,500
Guatemala	5,500
Nicaragua	3,200
Haiti	1,200

Source: *CIA World Factbook*, 2011

The Dominican Republic is a leading exporter of tropical organic produce. Large processing plants, such as this one on the north coast, hire skilled workers to oversee cocoa bean production.

IMPROVING INFRASTRUCTURE

Progress slowed dramatically due to inadequate infrastructure. Having too few power plants and poor roads, for example, hurt the economy by making it difficult for producers to manufacture and send their goods to markets.

Delivering electricity has been an ongoing, troublesome problem, as the blackout at the palace showed. This problem has several causes. In the 1980s, blackouts occurred because too few power plants existed. Aggravating the problem was the fact that the government owned the plants and ran them inefficiently. As industry grew, the demand for electricity rose. In response, the government encouraged **privatization**, the transfer of ownership from the government to the private sector. By 2003, privately run power companies finally had the capacity to produce sufficient power.

POWERING UP THE FUTURE

Yet the country's energy problems persisted. During the 2000s, global oil prices rose, and since power companies import oil to produce electricity, utility costs soared. Individuals and government agencies alike had trouble paying their electric bills. In addition, during the years when the government provided electricity, customers had grown accustomed to free service and now feel they should not have to pay for poor service. Consequently, electric companies have had less money to invest in capital improvements.

The Dominican Republic's leaders are seeking ways to solve the power problem soon. Improving supply and meeting demand will convince customers to pay for the power they use. Recently, the country's largest power company awarded a contract for a new plant to a manufacturer in Finland. Delivering more power efficiently will power the country strongly toward the future.

Explore the Issue

1. **Summarize** How has becoming a democracy helped the Dominican economy?

2. **Make Inferences** How will privatization of power plants improve standard of living in the Dominican Republic?

Locals and tourists fill the streets of a popular shopping district in Santo Domingo. To attract customers, the shops depend on reliable power.

LUXURY
IN THE UNITED

LUXURIOUS LIFESTYLE

What do you think of when you hear the word *luxury*? Does it bring to mind fast cars, large homes, costly electronics, or expensive trips?

Many people in the world describe luxury as something beyond what they need. In a recent lifestyle survey, one-third of respondents admitted that they feel guilty when they indulge in luxury. That response, however, is less typical in the United Arab Emirates, or UAE. (The word *emirate* comes from the historic title *emir*, which was used for a commander or prince.) Twenty-six percent of people surveyed in the UAE agree that luxury is a lifestyle to be enjoyed.

A worker operates a forklift at a refinery in the UAE. Millions of barrels of oil are exported to energy-hungry countries each year.

ARAB EMIRATES

LIQUID GOLD

With a population of just over 5 million people, the UAE had the eleventh highest GDP per capita in the world in 2011. Why do people in the UAE enjoy such a high standard of living? The answer is oil.

The UAE holds an enormous amount of petroleum, or crude oil, reserves. In 2011, a reliable estimate put reserves at 97.8 billion barrels. In an energy-hungry world, that's like owning liquid gold. As a large oil producer, the UAE is a member of OPEC, the Organization of the Petroleum Exporting Countries. OPEC works to coordinate oil production and distribution. Its members work together to increase their revenue from the sale of oil on the world market.

Dubai's prosperity attracts investors and visitors from all over the world.

FORMING A FEDERATION

The United Arab Emirates (UAE) enjoys a unique political structure, which grew out of its regional history and shared concerns. For centuries, the lands bordering the southern Persian Gulf and the Gulf of Oman were divided into small states ruled by sheikhs (SHEEKS), who were powerful Arab chiefs. In the 1800s, the states were unable to stop pirates from raiding ships. A treaty allowed the United Kingdom to maintain peace in those waters.

In the 1960s, the United Kingdom decided to give up its oversight of the area. The treaty ended on December 1, 1971, and the next day several of the small states formed a **federation**. A federation is formed when separate states unite under a central government. As in the United States, power is shared between states, called emirates, and the UAE federal government. A stable government helped the UAE take advantage of its oil reserves and prosperity followed.

RICH AND POOR

Although the UAE is a rich country, its wealth is not distributed evenly among its people. About 20 percent of the population lives in poverty. In addition, about 85 percent of laborers in the UAE are foreign workers who have few rights. Labor unions are illegal, so workers have little ability to pressure employers to improve conditions. Workers who go on strike can be deported.

The UAE experienced another economic problem which is related to real estate. Some emirates, including Dubai (doo-BY), had built luxury hotels and commercial developments. Then the global recession that began in 2008 hit the real estate sector especially hard. The value of property plummeted, dropping below the amounts developers owed. As a result, Dubai's debt increased and new buildings sat empty.

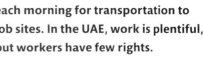

Foreign workers from Asia line up each morning for transportation to job sites. In the UAE, work is plentiful, but workers have few rights.

RECOVERY AND REFORM

In the UAE, regional political power is concentrated in the hands of a few; rulers are chosen because of their family and their position in their tribe. No political parties exist. Because a small group of people run the country, change is difficult to accomplish. Even so, political and social reforms are gradually being made. A few laws have been passed to help foreign workers, and the UAE held its first limited elections in December 2006.

To deal with the real estate crisis, the federal government took over some of Dubai's debt. In addition, Dubai worked out deals to restructure its debt, sold bonds to raise funds, and received a loan from emirate and UAE capital Abu Dhabi (AH boo DAH bee). In late 2011, the sheikh of Dubai expressed confidence that the crisis had passed.

PLANNING FOR THE FUTURE

As in the Dominican Republic, relying on only one sector of the economy for prosperity is risky. Oil prices can rise and fall rapidly, and such fluctuation makes it difficult to maintain a steady income or guarantee growth. Complicating matters is the fact that oil and natural gas are nonrenewable resources that will run out eventually. The oil and natural gas reserves of the UAE are projected to last another 150 years, but that is a relatively short amount of time in the history of a country.

The leaders of the UAE, however, are trying to diversify the economy by promoting manufacturing, banking, and tourism. In addition, the UAE has been placing emphasis on education as a way to improve its standard of living. More than three-fourths of the population is literate. By developing new industries and promoting education, the leaders of the UAE hope to afford luxury long after the oil wells run dry.

Explore the Issue

1. **Analyze** What changes might occur if the UAE were to diversify its economy?

2. **Synthesize** How might a broader political power base bring about positive economic changes in the UAE?

A sprawling new housing development lies unfinished on the outskirts of Dubai. When property values fell, many real estate developers delayed projects.

21

Providing Education Opportunities

Maasai children eagerly gather around teacher Kakenya Ntaiya to hear a humorous story.

EDUCATION FOR ALL

The Maasai (mah-SY) of East Africa have lived as nomads raising herds of cattle for hundreds of years, but the land can no longer adequately support their population. While the government of Kenya has encouraged the Maasai to settle in villages and on farms to help raise their low standard of living, that step alone is not enough to lift them out of poverty.

One reason is the lack of education opportunities. Although Kenya requires all children to attend school for at least eight years, many Maasai families take their daughters out of school at age 13 so they can marry. Traditionally, the Maasai have not encouraged girls or women to continue their education. A determined young Maasai girl, Kakenya Ntaiya (kah-KEN-yuh nuh-tuh-EE-yuh), challenged this practice. Ntaiya, who today is a National Geographic Emerging Explorer, has taken extraordinary steps to improve education for girls in Kenya.

In developing countries, educating women tends to raise the people's standard of living. Educated women often have fewer children, which reduces overpopulation. **Overpopulation**—the condition of having more people than an area can support—is one of the numerous reasons for low standards of living in many developing countries around the world.

A YOUNG GIRL'S DREAM

Born in a small Kenyan village, Ntaiya was the first of eight children in a family with a father who worked in a distant city and a mother who labored in sugarcane fields. As the oldest child in the family, Ntaiya had to help with all the chores, work in the fields, and care for her siblings.

When Ntaiya turned five, her parents announced her engagement to a village boy. This was the custom among traditional people in Kenya. But as a young girl, Ntaiya dreamed of becoming a teacher, and so she negotiated with her parents to be allowed to attend high school. In exchange for their permission, she promised to follow Maasai customs and study hard to earn good grades. True to her promise, Ntaiya achieved high grades and won a college scholarship to study in the United States. She looked forward to the exciting opportunity.

KEEPING A PROMISE

As Ntaiya prepared for college, her father became ill and could not work. The family had no money to send Ntaiya overseas. Again she negotiated, this time with a village leader, promising to use her education to help her people. The village worked hard to raise the money to send her to college, and Ntaiya kept her promise.

Ntaiya attended graduate school to earn an advanced degree in education, and she also worked to achieve an ambitious plan—to build a girls' school in her village. In 2009, she opened the Academy for Girls, the first primary school for girls in that part of Kenya.

"I'm helping girls who cannot speak for themselves," Ntaiya explains. "Why should they go through the hardships I endured? They'll be stepping on my shoulders to move up the ladder—they're not going to start on the bottom."

In its first two years, the Academy enrolled 60 students. Ntaiya's goal is to increase the enrollment to 150 students in grades four through eight. "We keep class sizes very small, so each girl receives a great deal of individual attention," Ntaiya says.

MAKING A DIFFERENCE

Kakenya Ntaiya raises money for her school by accepting invitations to speak with helping organizations all over the world. On her trips abroad, she shares the story of one girl's promise to her people. Because Ntaiya believes that education will empower the girls and their families, she is helping the Maasai shape a brighter future for themselves.

Kakenya Ntaiya succeeds because she set goals and works hard to achieve them. You, too, can set worthwhile goals and use your skills to make a difference in your world. The activity on the next two pages gives you a way to start.

Explore the Issue

1. **Draw Conclusions** Why is it important to educate Maasai girls beyond elementary school?

2. **Make Predictions** How might the work of Kakenya Ntaiya affect the standard of living of her people?

Kakenya Ntaiya shares a new book with Maasai children who are learning to read.

Organize
a Food Drive
—and report your results

People in need are everywhere, not just in countries with low standards of living. Most communities have one or more food banks, places that collect and distribute food to people in need. Organize a food drive in your school, and donate the food to a community food bank. You'll be sharing food with people who really need it.

RESEARCH

- Find out the name, location, and phone number of a food bank in your community.
- Call the food bank to find out what kinds of food items they collect and to ask about their hours of operation.
- Make a list of the food you plan to collect. Be sure to include locally grown produce and products.

ORGANIZE

- Prepare a flyer announcing your food drive and indicating the date that you want students to bring their donations to school.
- Make copies of the flyers, and distribute them to students and teachers in all the classes at your school.
- Obtain large boxes, label them, and place them in each classroom before the day of the food drive.

Community volunteers make a difference by serving meals to those in need.

DELIVER

- Collect all the boxes of donated food.

- Ask volunteers to help inventory and organize the food into bags and boxes that can be carried efficiently.

- Call the food bank and arrange the best time to deliver the food.

- Line up volunteers and adults at school to help load and transport the donated food to the food bank.

SHARE

- Announce the results of your food drive on your school's intercom, telling how many boxes of food you collected.

- Write a letter to your community newspaper, describing your efforts and encouraging others to donate to the food bank.

- Interview the director of the food bank to ask about the number of people it serves and peak times of need. Then present your findings to other classes at school.

Research &
WRITE
Argument

Write an Argumentative Article

What action would you like to see people take to improve the standard of living in the United States? Promote bicycling to improve our health? Increase the number of teacher aides to give individual attention to students who need help? Your task is to identify a way to improve our standard of living and to write a convincing argument promoting your claim.

RESEARCH

Use the Internet, books, and articles to find the following information:

- Data on the standard of living in the United States
- Suggested actions to improve the standard of living
- Evidence to support these suggestions

As you do your research, be sure to take good notes and document your sources.

DRAFT

Review your notes and identify a course of action that you will recommend to others. It may be one you've researched, or it may be your own idea. Then write a draft.

- The first paragraph, or introduction, should get the reader's attention; present your course of action, which is also known as your claim; and state your reasons for supporting this course of action.
- The second paragraph, or body, should provide logical reasons and relevant evidence supporting your claim that this course of action will help raise the standard of living. Use accurate, credible sources for your evidence.
- The third paragraph, or conclusion, should provide a statement that follows from and supports the argument you presented.

REVISE & EDIT

Read your first draft to make sure that you make and support your claim with logical reasons and relevant evidence.

- Does the introduction get the attention of your audience and introduce your topic clearly?
- Does the body use words, phrases, and clauses that clarify the relationships among the claim, reasons, and evidence?
- Does your concluding statement follow from and support your argument?

Revise the article to make sure you have established logical relationships among the claim, the reasons, and the evidence. Be sure you have presented your argument in a logical order, and then check your paper for errors in spelling and punctuation. Save your work.

PUBLISH & PRESENT

Now you are ready to publish and present your article. Add any images or graphs that enhance your ideas, and prepare a source list.

Then print out your article, or write a clean copy by hand. Post it in the classroom or on your class website.

Visual GLOSSARY

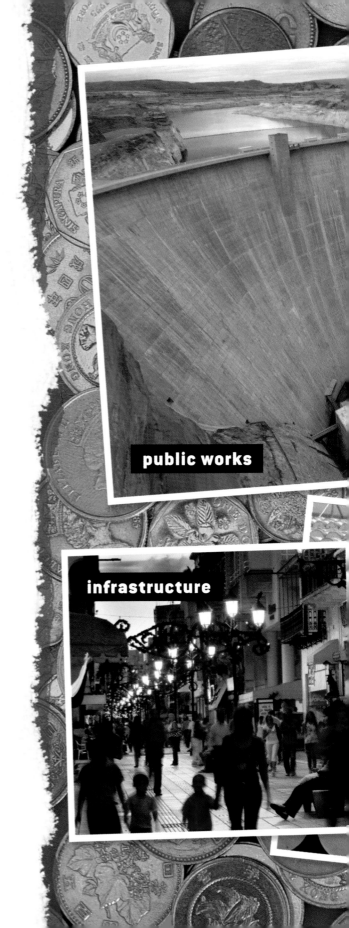

cost of living *n.*, the amount of money required to maintain a certain standard of living

diversify *v.*, to develop more economic sectors

federation *n.*, separate states united under one central government

GDP per capita *n.*, the total value of all goods and services produced in a country in a year, divided by population

income gap *n.*, difference in average wages between rich and poor

infrastructure *n.*, the system of public works that supports modern life

life expectancy *n.*, the number of years that a person in a particular group or place can expect to live

overpopulation *n.*, the condition of having more people than an area can support

poverty line *n.*, the minimum income required to meet basic needs

privatization *n.*, the transfer from governmental to private ownership

public works *n.*, government constructed projects for public use

sector *n.*, one segment of an economy, such as agriculture or oil

standard of living *n.*, the level of available income, goods, and services

public works

infrastructure

cost of living

standard of living

sector

INDEX

SKILLS